Family Treasures from DEVRA'S KITCHEN

Devra Berkowitz

HALLARD
PRESS

Cover Design, Typography & Production
by Hallard Press LLC/John W Prince

Cover Photo: Howard Barman

Published by Hallard Press LLC.
www.HallardPress.com   Info@HallardPress.com
352-234-6099
Bulk copies of this book can be ordered at Info@HallardPress.com

Publisher's Cataloging-in-Publication data

Names: Berkowitz, Devra, author.
Title: Family treasures from Devra's kitchen / Devra Berkowitz.
Description: The Villages, FL: Hallard Press, 2021.
Identifiers: LCCN: 2021925919 | ISBN: 978-1-951188-42-9 (Hardcover) | ISBN: 978-1-951188-47-4 (Paperback)
Subjects: LCSH Jewish cooking. | Kosher food. | Cookbooks. | BISAC COOKING / Regional & Ethnic / Jewish & Kosher | COOKING / Regional & Ethnic / American / General | COOKING / Cooking for Kids
Classification: LCC TX724 .B462 2022 | DDC 641.5/676--dc23

Printed in the United States of America

ISBN: 978-1-951188-42-9 (Hardcover)
ISBN: 978-1-951188-47-4 (Paperback)

Dedicated with Love to

Grandma Celia Berkowitz
Grandma Jane Gabriel
Nana Carmella "Carmen" Sylvester
Aunt Ida Youngerman
and, of course, my family.

Cooking is an Art;
Baking is a Science.

Cooking is the art of blending ingredients together to create a pleasing taste and texture. So we can take a "splash" of this and a "dash" of that and an amount of "to taste" for something else. Cooks soon learn from experience how much is in a "rounded tablespoon." It takes some additional work to mess up cooking.

Baking is a science where fairly exacting amounts of various ingredients are mixed and then heated so that a chemical reaction takes place and the goopy concoction in the bowl becomes cake. Mess up the measurements and strange things can happen—most of them inedible.

One of the culinary skills I teach everyone is to "have fun in the kitchen." It's fun to experiment, try new recipes, and variations on old recipes.

Here are a selection of my well-tested everyday recipes— tried and true, but certainly family and friends' favorites—some handed down for generations, and others more recently contributed to add to the flavor.

I hope that you have lots of fun with them.

Devra Berkowitz
November 2021

RECIPES

APPETIZERS & STARTERS 9
   Vegetable Dip 10
   Baked Brie 10
   Crab on Toast 11
   Cheese and Apple Spread 11
   Barbequed Chicken Wings (Hot Wings) 12
   Lemon Flank Steak Skewers 13
   Spanakopita Triangles 14
   Swedish Meatballs 16
   Nut Berry Cheese Ball 17

BREADS 19
   Vienna Christmas Fruit Bread 20
   Banana Bread 21
   Challah 22
   Date and Nut Bread 23
   Zucchini Bread 24
   Rich Crescent Rolls 25
   Plain Crescent Rolls 26
   Dad's Favorite Date Nut Bread 27
   Southern Buttermilk Biscuits 28
   Granny's Biscuits 29
   Soft Buttermilk Dinner Rolls 30

MAINS, SALADS, SIDES & SAUCES 31
   Baked Ziti 32
   Beef Stew 33
   Chili Con Carne 34
   Beef Brisket 36
   Corned Beef (alone or with cabbage) 37

Chicken Creole 38
Barbecue Chicken (Sweet & Sour) 40
Chicken Soup 42
Matzo Balls 43
Chicken Rice Casserole 44
Medium White Sauce 45
Eggplant and Ground Meat Parmigiana 47
Italian Meatballs 48
Spaghetti Sauce (Gravy) 49
Tuna Noodle Casserole 50
Sweet Potato Casserole 51
Thanksgiving Stuffing 52
Seasoning Mix 52
Marinated Mushrooms 53
Stuffed Cabbage 54
Corn Pudding 55
Vegetable Marinade 56
Mom's Cucumber Salad 57
Bread and Butter Pickles (A Canadian Treat) 58
Marinade for Steak 59
Creamed Chicken (Chicken a la King) 60
Grape Salad 61
Shrimp & Grits 62

SWEETS & DESSERTS 63
Blueberry Tea Cake 64
Chocolate Cake (Sour Cream) 65
Mother's Cheese Cake 66
Chocolate Éclair Cake 68
Delicious Coffee Cake 69
Honey Cake 70
Pineapple Cake 71
Cream Cheese Frosting 71
Delicious White Cake 72

Schnecken 73
Rich Yellow Cake 74
Fudge Brownies 75
Decorator's Frosting 76
Decorator's Fudge Frosting 77
Toll House Cookies 78
Cookie Press Cookies 79
Angie's Cookies/Biscotti 80
Ginger Snaps 81
Half Moon Cookies 82
Molasses Raisin Cookies 83
Refrigerator Cookies 84
Never Fail Strudel 85
Rugelach (Parve) 86
Rugelach Dough (Dairy) 87
Strawberry Pie 88
Pumpkin Pie 89
Rice Pudding 90
Chocoholic's Dutch Cocoa Mix 91
Kentucky Bourbon Balls 92
Dipping Chocolate 93
Buckeyes 94
Lemon-Blueberry Dutch Baby 95
Chocolate Cherry Heart Smart Cookies .. 96
Broye du Poitou 97
Blueberry Cobbler 98
Blackberry Cobbler 99
Red Velvet Layer Cake 100
Cream Cheese Frosting 100
Jewish Apple Cake 102
5-Minute Chocolate Butter Cream Frosting 103

JEWISH HOLIDAY 105
Carrot Tzimmes 106

Knoedle 107
Aunt Ida's Taiglach 108
Grandma Jane's Taiglach 109
Luckshion Kugel (Noodles) 110
Blintz Souffle 111
Cheese Blintzes 112
Potato Kugel 113
Potato Latkes 114
Passover Sponge Cake 115

BABY & KIDS 117
Baby's Health Crackers 118
Teething Biscuits 119
Homemade Play Dough 120
Play Clay 121

Author Biography **123**

Appendix: Alphabetical recipe list **124**

"*Devra's Kitchen* ensures that many people will now be able to experience Devra's remarkable cooking."
—Suzanne and Tom Drumm (Virginia)

Appetizers & Starters

VEGETABLE DIP

INGREDIENTS:

1 8-ounce container non fat plain yogurt

1 cup mayonnaise

1 tablespoon each dill, beau monde and chopped green chives

Combine all ingredients in bowl. Mix well. Cover and refrigerate.

Serve with assorted vegetables.

Note: recipe can be stored covered in refrigerator up to 3 weeks. It makes a nice salad dressing. Recipe is easily doubled.

BAKED BRIE

INGREDIENTS:

Phyllo dough (about half the package for baby wheel)

Wheel of brie

Encase brie in dough and pinch at seams. Bake at 375° for 20-30 minutes. Remove from oven and let stand 5 minutes.

Serve with crackers and apple, or cranberry. Top with a sprig of parsley for color.

CRAB ON TOAST

INGREDIENTS:

1 8-ounce can lump crab
½ cup mayonnaise
1 cup shredded Swiss cheese
1½ teaspoons garlic powder
1 French baguette sliced into ¼" thick pieces

Combine first 4 ingredients. Arrange sliced bread on cookie sheet and lightly toast.Top with crab mixture and bake or broil until cheese is melted. Extra cheese can be added to top before melting if desired.

Serve hot.

CHEESE AND APPLE SPREAD

INGREDIENTS:

8 ounce package (brick) cream cheese, softened
½ cup mayonnaise
½ cup shredded natural sharp cheddar cheese
½ cup finely chopped apples

Combine softened cream cheese and mayonnaise until well blended.Add cheddar cheese and apples; mix well and chill.

Serve with apple wedges, crackers or bread.

BARBEQUED CHICKEN WINGS (HOT WINGS)

INGREDIENTS:

30 Ounces Durkee's Hot Sauce

1 pound butter

2 tablespoons garlic powder

2 ounces Worcestershire sauce

7 drops Tabasco sauce (or to taste)

10-15 pounds chicken wings cut apart

Melt all ingredients together, except wings, in a pan on the stove over low heat.

Prepare wings if using fresh whole ones. Place fresh or frozen wing parts on cooling rack which has been placed on double foil lined cookie sheets or jelly roll pans. Bake in 350° oven 30-45 minutes for fresh or thawed wings: 1-1¼ hours for frozen wings. Wings should be tender and light brown (NOT CRISP)

Remove wings from racks, remove racks and top layer of foil from pans; dip wings in sauce and place on foil lined pans. Baste with additional sauce so they are WELL covered before returning to oven.

Bake another 30-45 minutes until crisp turning as needed to prevent burning and basting if they appear dry but not crisp.

Note: May take up to 2 hours to thoroughly crisp. Be sure to defrost wings before cooking to keep crisping time to max of 2 hours.

LEMON FLANK STEAK SKEWERS

INGREDIENTS:

2/3 cup olive oil

4 teaspoons lemon zest

½ cup fresh lemon juice

2 teaspoons salt

½ teaspoon dried crushed red pepper

4 (2 pound) flank steaks, cut diagonally into ¼ inch thick slices

50 (12 inch) wooden skewers

Combine first 5 ingredients in a shallow dish or heavy-duty zip-top plastic bag; add steak. Cover or seal, and chill 8 hours, turning occasionally.

Place skewers in water to cover, and let soak 10 minutes. (Can place meat on dry skewers prior to marinating.)

Remove steak from marinade, discarding marinade.

Thread each steak slice onto 1 skewer.

Grill skewers, covered with grill lid, over medium-high heat (350°-400°) 4 to 5 minutes on each side or to desired degree of doneness.

SPANAKOPITA TRIANGLES

INGREDIENTS:

1 10-ounce package frozen chopped spinach, thawed and squeezed dry

4 ounces feta cheese, crumbled

1 egg white

1 clove garlic, minced

¼ teaspoon salt

¼ teaspoon freshly ground black pepper

1/8 teaspoon nutmeg

12 sheets thawed frozen phyllo dough

olive oil flavored cooking spray

In a medium-sized bowl, combine spinach, cheese, egg white, garlic, salt, pepper, and nutmeg; mix well. Arrange one sheet of phyllo dough on work surface; coat with cooking spray. Arrange another sheet directly over first sheet; coat with cooking spray. Repeat with one more sheet. Cut phyllo stack lengthwise into 3" wide strips.

Place a heaping tablespoon of spinach mixture at one end of the first strip about 1 inch from the edge. Fold the corner over it to make a triangle. Continue until whole strip is folded into a triangular packet. Coat the packet with cooking spray. Repeat procedure until all spinach mixture and phyllo dough is used. (If desired, freeze the triangles in a freezer bag for up to three weeks before baking.)

Preheat oven to 375°. Arrange triangles in a single layer on baking sheet coated with cooking spray. Bake 16-18 minutes (20 minutes if triangles are frozen) or until golden brown.

Serve warm or at room temperature. (Triangles may be baked up to one day ahead and refrigerated. Reheat in a 350° oven, 10-12 minutes.)

SWEDISH MEATBALLS

INGREDIENTS:

2 pounds ground beef
1 cup bread crumbs
½ teaspoon onion salt
½ teaspoon garlic salt
scant ¼ teaspoon black pepper
1/3 cup water
¼ cup raisins
¼ cup brown sugar
2 cups beef bouillon
½ cup water
1 can tomato sauce (6 oz size)
lemon juice to taste

Mix ground beef, onion salt, garlic salt, pepper, bread crumbs and 1/3 cup water together. Form mixture into balls the size of walnuts and brown in deep oil.

(Place oil to a depth of 1½ inches in a 3 quart sauce pan browning 12 meatballs at a time.) Set meatballs aside on paper towel lined plate.

In a large sauce pan combine tomato sauce, beef bouillon, brown sugar, raisins, ½ cup water and lemon juice. Heat this to boil; add meatballs and cook 35-45 minutes at boil.

Place in chafing dish and serve with toothpicks.

NUT BERRY
CHEESE BALL

INGREDIENTS:

8 ounces cream cheese
2 ounces crumbled blue cheese
8 ounces sun-dried cranberries
8 ounces pistachio nuts, chopped
½ cup butter
4 ounces brie, rind removed

Mix nuts and cranberries, reserve 2 tablespoons for garnish.

Mix all cheeses and butter until smooth.

Line a small bowl or mold with plastic wrap and layer 1/3 of cheese mixture at bottom. Layer 1/3 of nut/berry mixture; continue layering ending with nut/berry mixture.

Chill for several hours or overnight. Unmold and garnish with reserved nut/berry mixture.

Serve with ginger snaps, Moravian spice crackers, bagel chips, etc.

NOTES

"I've tasted many of Devra's recipes and highly recommend her cookbook"
—Robert Tetrault, Florida

Breads

VIENNA CHRISTMAS FRUIT BREAD

INGREDIENTS:

8 large eggs
1½ cups golden raisins
2 cups sugar
1½ cups chopped walnuts or pecans
4-1/3 cups flour
¾ cup candied fruits
4 teaspoons baking powder
1 tablespoon grated lemon rind
½ cup brandy
2 teaspoons vanilla extract

Beat the eggs and sugar for 10 minutes with an electric mixer. Fold in 4 cups of the flour and the baking powder. Combine rest of ingredients with the remaining 1/3 cup flour and add to the mixture, folding in gently.

Pour into 2 large or 6 mini buttered loaf pans and let stand at room temperature for 20 minutes. Bake in a 325° oven for 1 hour, or until loaves test done. To prevent over browning, place loaves on the lower shelf of the oven.

BANANA BREAD

(LAURIE BERKOWITZ)

INGREDIENTS:

3 mashed bananas

¾ cup sugar

½ cup oil

2 eggs

2 teaspoons baking powder

½ teaspoon salt

2 cups sifted flour

½ cup finely chopped nuts (optional)

1 teaspoon baking soda dissolved in 1 tablespoon cold water

Cream together sugar and shortening. Add well beaten eggs and mashed bananas. Add baking powder, salt and baking soda. Mix in flour and add nuts. Pour into greased pans and bake at 325° for 45-50 minutes. Cool and store.

NOTE: Can be baked as muffins with baking time 28-30 minutes.

CHALLAH
(AUNT IDA YOUNGERMAN)

INGREDIENTS:

2 cakes yeast (or 1 dry yeast pkg, or 2¼ tsp dry yeast)

2 cups warm water

1/3 cup sugar

4 teaspoons salt

¼ cup oil

7½ - 8 cups flour

3 slightly beaten eggs (save some egg for brushing on top before baking)

Soften yeast in ½ cup water in a warm small bowl. Add 1 teaspoon sugar; let stand 10 minutes. Pour this mixture into remaining 1½ cups warm water. Add sugar, salt, oil and beaten eggs; blend well. Add 3 cups flour and blend. Add rest of flour until quite a stiff dough is formed. Let rest on floured board for 10 minutes then knead for about 5-6 minutes. Put in a greased bowl, cover and let rise 1½ hours. Cut into thirds; knead each third a few times then divide it into 3 equal parts. Roll each part into a rope approximately 1" in diameter. Braid to form challah. Repeat with remaining dough to form 2 more loaves.

Place loaves on greased cookie sheet or in individual greased loaf pans. Let rise 45-60 minutes. Brush with remaining egg

Bake in 375° oven 40-45 minutes until top is golden brown.

NOTE: If desired can form into one huge loaf by placing 2 loaves side by side on cookie sheet and the third on top of this. Brush with egg mixture. Place aluminum foil down the sides just before placing in oven; remove foil after first 10 minutes of baking.

DATE AND NUT BREAD

(JANE GABRIEL)

INGREDIENTS:

1 pound dates, cut up
½ cup boiling water
1¾ cup sugar
1½ teaspoon salt
1 egg
2¾ cups flour
2 tablespoons butter
1 tablespoon vanilla
1 cup chopped nuts

Mix together dates and boiling water, set aside to cool. Cream sugar, egg and butter together. Add remaining ingredients and mix well. Add cooled date mixture and mix. Pour into 3 small or 2 large loaf pans. Bake in 350° oven for 1 hour.

ZUCCHINI BREAD

INGREDIENTS:

3 eggs
1 teaspoon baking soda
1 cup oil
1 teaspoon baking powder
2 cups sugar
3 cups flour
2 cups unpeeled, grated zucchini
1 teaspoon salt
2 teaspoons vanilla
2 teaspoons cinnamon
chopped nuts if desired

Beat eggs

Add oil, sugar, zucchini and vanilla.

Mix well; add dry ingredients and mix.

Add nuts if desired and mix again. Pour into 2 greased loaf pans. Bake at 350° for 50-55 minutes.

RICH CRESCENT ROLLS

INGREDIENTS:

1 cup sugar

½ cup soft shortening, butter or margarine

1 teaspoon salt

2 eggs

¾ cup lukewarm milk

2 cakes compressed yeast (or 1 dry yeast package, or 2¼ tsp dry yeast)

4 cups sifted flour

Mix first 4 ingredients together until smooth (use rotary beater if desired). Stir in milk, crumble yeast if cake, or sprinkle if dry, over mixture and stir until dissolved. Using a spoon, beat in flour adding it slowly. Scrape dough from sides of bowl, cover with damp cloth and let rise until double, approximately 1½ hours.

Place on lightly floured board and roll to ¼ to ½ inch thickness. Cut to shape into crescents or butter horns. Place on baking sheet and cover. Let rise until double, approximately 1 hour.

Bake in 425° oven until golden brown (about 12-15 minutes). Yields 20 rolls.

PLAIN CRESCENT ROLLS

INGREDIENTS:

2 tablespoons sugar

6 tablespoons soft shortening, butter or margarine

1½ cups lukewarm milk

2 cakes compressed yeast (or 1 package dry, or 2¼ tsp dry yeast)

4 cups sifted flour

Mix together first 3 ingredients until smooth (use rotary beater if desired). Stir in milk, crumble yeast over mixture and stir until dissolved. Using a spoon beat in flour, adding it slowly. Scrape dough from sides of bowl, cover with damp cloth and let rise until double, approximately 30 minutes.

Place on lightly floured board and roll to ¼ to ½ inch thickness. Cut to shape into crescents or butter horns. Place on baking sheet and cover. Let rise until double, approximately 15 minutes.

Bake in 425° oven until golden brown (about 12-15 minutes). Yields about 24 rolls.

DAD'S FAVORITE DATE NUT BREAD

(BARBARA TAGG)

INGREDIENTS:

¾ cup chopped nuts

1 cup chopped dates

1½ teaspoon baking soda

½ teaspoon salt

¼ cup shortening

¾ cup boiling water

2 eggs

½ teaspoon vanilla

1 cup sugar

1½ cups flour

Combine nuts, dates, soda, and salt in a mixing bowl. Add shortening and boiling water. Stir to blend. Allow to sit for 15 minutes.

Beat eggs lightly. Add vanilla. Stir in sugar and flour. Add to date mixture. Do not overmix. Place in greased bread pan.

Bake 1 hour at 350°.

SOUTHERN BUTTERMILK BISCUITS

(LAUREN CONNOR BERKOWITZ)

INGREDIENTS:

½ cup cold butter, cubed
2 cups self-rising flour*
¾ cup buttermilk

Preheat oven to 425°.

In a large bowl, cut butter into flour until mixture resembles coarse crumbs. Stir in buttermilk until moistened. Turn onto lightly floured surface; knead 3-4 times. Pat or lightly roll into ¾ inch thickness. Cut with a 2½ inch biscuit cutter.

Place on greased baking sheet. Bake until golden brown, 11-13 minutes. Brush tops with butter. Serve warm.

*NOTE: If you do not have self-rising flour, combine 2 cups all-purpose flour with 1 tablespoon baking POWDER and ½ teaspoon salt.

GRANNY'S BISCUITS

INGREDIENTS:

2 cups all-purpose flour

1 tablespoon baking POWDER

1/3 cup shortening (butter, margarine, solid Crisco)

2/3 cup 2% milk

1 large egg, lightly beaten

Preheat oven to 450°.

In a large bowl, whisk flour, baking powder, and salt. Cut in shortening until mixture resembles coarse crumbs. Add milk; stir until moistened.

Turn onto a lightly floured surface; knead 8 -10 times. Pat dough into a 10" x 14" rectangle. Cut rectangle in half lengthwise; cut crosswise to make 10 squares.

Place 1" apart on UNGREASED baking sheet; brush tops with egg.

Bake until golden brown, 8 -10 minutes. Serve warm.

SOFT BUTTERMILK DINNER ROLLS

INGREDIENTS:

1 package (1/4 oz) active dry yeast

¼ cup warm water (110° to 115°)

1 cup plus 2 tablespoons warm buttermilk (110° to 115°) divided

½ cup plus 2 teaspoons butter, divided

1 large egg, room temperature

1/3 cup sugar

1 teaspoon salt

4 cups bread flour

Dissolve yeast in warm water until foamy. In a large bowl, combine 1 cup buttermilk, ½ cup butter, egg, sugar, salt, and yeast mixture. Add 3 cups flour and beat on medium speed until smooth, 1 minute. Add remaining flour, ¼ cup at a time, to form a soft dough.

Turn dough onto a lightly floured surface; knead until smooth and elastic, 6-8 minutes. Place in a greased bowl, turning once to grease the top. Cover and let rise in a warm place until doubled, about 1 hour.

Punch down dough. Turn onto a lightly floured surface; divide and shape into 20 balls. Place in a greased 13" x 9" pan. Cover with a kitchen towel; let rise in a warm place until almost doubled, about 45 minutes.

Preheat oven to 350°. Brush rolls lightly with remaining buttermilk and butter. Bake until golden brown, 20-25 minutes. Cool in pan 20 minutes. Remove to wire rack; serve warm.

Mains,
Salads,
Sides,
& Sauces

BAKED ZITI

INGREDIENTS:

1 pound ziti macaroni
12 ounces shredded mozzarella cheese
Parmesan and Romano grated blend
1 jar spaghetti sauce or 1 quart homemade sauce

Cook ziti per package instructions until tender, (or as desired) about 10 minutes, drain. In casserole or square baking pan place sauce to coat bottom, layer of ziti, more sauce, and a layer of mozzarella cheese, sprinkle with Parmesan and Romano. Repeat layers until all pasta used, ending with scant layer of sauce (you can see cheese through the sauce).

Bake in a 350° oven 25-30 minutes until bubbly and cheese melted.

NOTE: If sauce is very thick, thin with small amount of water. If casserole appears dry when assembling, add a few tablespoons water at edges after assembled.

BEEF STEW

(GRANDMA CELIA [CELE] BERKOWITZ)

INGREDIENTS:

1-1½ pounds stew beef

1 large can tomatoes

1 medium onion, diced

¾ carrots sliced

2 stalks celery (chopped)

1 cup potatoes (cubed)

½ tsp salt, ¼ tsp pepper, ¾-1 cup flour to dredge meat

Combine flour, salt, and pepper.

Flour meat and brown in hot oil (just enough to cover bottom of 4-5 quart Dutch oven). Brown meat a little at a time removing to paper towel lined plate to drain as each batch finishes.

Remove pan from heat; scrape bottom to loosen bits of flour. Place onion, carrots, and celery on bottom; return meat to pan placing over vegetables. Pour in canned tomatoes with juice adding enough water to cover meat. Add a good squirt of ketchup, a splash of A-1 and 2 splashes of Worcestershire sauce (or to taste). Cook 2-3 hours over medium heat stirring occasionally. Put potatoes in for last hour of cooking.

NOTE: Potatoes can be peeled and diced during prep and kept in water until needed.

CHILI CON CARNE

(DEVRA BERKOWITZ)

INGREDIENTS:

2 medium onions (sliced)

1 cup chopped green pepper (1 large)

1 tablespoon chilli powder

1-28 ounce can tomatoes

2-15.5 ounce cans kidney beans, rinsed and drained

1 pound ground beef

Cook and stir ground beef, onion, and green peppers in large skillet or Dutch oven until meat is brown and onion is tender.

Drain off fat and, if using a skillet, place ingredients in pot or slow cooker.

IF IN POT: add all remaining ingredients EXCEPT kidney beans. Heat to boiling, reduce heat, cover and simmer 2 hours, stirring occasionally. Stir in kidney beans and continue cooking at least 20 minutes before serving.

IF IN SLOW COOKER: add ALL ingredients (including kidney beans) and cover. Cook on low for 6 hours.

Taste and adjust spicing as needed at end of cooking time.

(SETH BERKOWITZ'S VARIATION)

Add the following to taste when chilli powder is added:

Cumin

Oregano

Paprika (Hot, Hungarian, or regular)

6 drops of Tabasco sauce

Brown beef in fry pay and drain.

Place all ingredients in crock pot and cook on low 6-8 hours.

(MARA NEBOSHYNSKY'S VARIATION)

INGREDIENTS:

1 pound ground beef

2-3 pounds large fresh ripe plum tomatoes

3-4 large jalapeno peppers, seeded and chopped

1 can kidney beans, rinsed and drained

2 medium onions diced

Brown beef in fry pan and drain.

Place all ingredients in crock pot and cook on low 6-8 hours.

BEEF BRISKET

INGREDIENTS:

3-4 pounds brisket (double deckle preferred)
4 carrots
2 pounds potatoes
1 medium onion
water

Clean carrots and potatoes and cut into chunks. Dice onion and place in bottom of foil lined roasting pan.

Season brisket with seasoning mix (recipe on page 52) and place over onion. Arrange potatoes and carrots around meat. Add water to cover bottom and come ½ way up meat. Cover pan with foil and seal edges.

Bake in 350° oven 3 hours or until meat is fork tender. If desired remove cover last ½ hour to brown potatoes.

NOTE: Tastes better cooked the day before and reheated.

CORNED BEEF

(WITH CABBAGE)

INGREDIENTS:

1 bay leaf

¾ teaspoon pickling spices

3 whole cloves

1½ cups water

3-4 pound corned beef (preferably brisket)

1 small head cabbage if desired

Combine all ingredients except corned beef and cabbage in crock pot.

Add corned beef fat side up. Cover and cook on Low setting 10-12 hours or until fork tender. (On high setting cook 5-6 hours.)

When corned beef is tender remove from pot to platter and cover with foil. Add cabbage which has been cut into wedges, cover and cook on high until fork tender (about 30 minutes).

SPICY CHICKEN CREOLE

INGREDIENTS:

4 whole chicken breasts, skinless and boneless
2 tablespoons oil
1 cup onion, sliced thin
2 cups mushrooms, sliced thin (1-8 oz container)
2 tablespoons garlic, minced
1 cup celery, chopped
1 tablespoon oregano
1 tablespoon basil
2 cups green pepper, sliced
1 large can diced tomatoes (28 oz can)
½ cup dry white wine (I usually use White
    Zinfandel)
2 tablespoons lemon juice
¼ teaspoon crushed hot red pepper
1 tablespoon margarine
freshly ground black pepper

Split chicken breast in half lengthwise; cut into ½ inch cubes and set aside.

For Creole sauce: heat oil in a large skillet, sauté onion until transparent. Add mushrooms and cook over medium heat until liquid evaporates; then add garlic, celery and spices and cook for 1 minute. Add green pepper and cook for 2 minutes. Stir in tomatoes and cook for about 5 minutes. Add wine, lemon juice, hot pepper and mix. Set aside.

In another skillet, heat half the margarine. Add half the chicken and sprinkle with black pepper. Cook over high heat, stirring frequently, until pieces are evenly and lightly browned. Do not over cook. Transfer chicken to separate dish. Repeat procedure for remaining chicken and then return the first batch to the skillet.

Pour Creole sauce over all and stir gently to blend. Simmer together for about 1 minute.

Serve over rice.

NOTE: *This is even better when cooked ahead and reheated.*

BARBECUE CHICKEN

(SWEET AND SOUR CHICKEN)

(BARBARA TAGG)

INGREDIENTS:
Marinade
3 cups white vinegar
3½ teaspoons salt
1½ teaspoons prepared mustard
4½ tablespoons ketchup
9 tablespoons lemon juice
black pepper to taste

Browning Sauce
6 tablespoons sugar
1½ teaspoons salt
9 tablespoons butter
3½ tablespoons prepared mustard
3½ teaspoons Worcestershire sauce
¼ teaspoon black pepper
4-2 pound chickens (cut into pieces) OR 8
  pounds chicken parts (breasts, thighs and drum
  sticks)

Mix marinade ingredients together and set aside.

Pierce chicken and place in shallow pan; pour marinade over them, cover with foil and refrigerate over night. Turn pieces and continue to marinate at least 4 hours longer.

Place covered pan of chicken and marinade in oven and turn on to 350°. Bake for 25 minutes after oven has heated to 350°

While chicken is baking, place all browning sauce ingredients in small sauce pan over low heat. Once butter has melted stir to mix and turn off burner.

Heat grill. Remove chicken pieces from baking pan one at a time, brush with browning sauce and place bony side down. Cook 25 minutes basting frequently with browning sauce and turning as needed to prevent burning.

NOTE: Any remaining browning sauce may be heated and served as gravy if desired.

CHICKEN SOUP

INGREDIENTS:

5 pound stewing chicken
1 tablespoon salt
1 medium onion
3 large carrots (sliced)
2-3 stalks celery
about 3 quarts water

Trim off as much fat as possible from chicken. (Leave skin on for better flavor.) Wash chicken and put in large stock pot with salt and onion; add water, being sure it covers chicken. Bring to boil and skim off foam. Place carrots in cheese cloth sack*; add carrots and celery to pot. Simmer until chicken is tender.

Remove chicken to plate. Remove sack of carrots and set aside. Strain soup discarding celery and onion. Slice carrots; return broth and carrots to pot.

Serve with noodles, rice or matzo balls.

NOTE: To make a cheesecloth sack, cut two 18" lengths of cheesecloth. Open each to a single layer and place onion and celery in one; carrots in the other. Bring corners of square together at center and tie with string or heavy thread.

MATZO BALLS

INGREDIENTS:

1 cup matzo meal or matzo ball mix
4 eggs, beaten
½ cup water
1/3 cup oil
1 teaspoon salt
dash of pepper

Add water, oil, salt and pepper to the beaten eggs and mix well. Add matzo meal and stir thoroughly; refrigerate one hour.

Dampen hands with water and form into balls about 1" in diameter. Drop into boiling soup or 1½ quarts boiling water to which 1 tablespoon salt has been added. Cover and cook 20 minutes. Do NOT peek.

CHICKEN RICE CASSEROLE

INGREDIENTS:

2 or 3 boneless, skinless chicken breasts
2 cups white wine (I use Zinfandel)
2 cups uncooked rice (regular, NOT instant)
1 can cream of chicken soup (10 oz size)
1 bag frozen California mix vegetables
2 cups water

Place water and wine in medium pot; add chicken and cook covered over medium heat until chicken is tender. Remove chicken to plate. Measure liquid for use in cooking rice, reserve ½ cup to thin soup.

Cook rice according to package directions using liquid from chicken (add water to get the required amount of liquid if needed).

While rice is cooking, cut chicken into bite size pieces and cook vegetables in microwave per package directions.

When rice is cooked mix with chicken, thinned soup and vegetables together to blend. Place in casserole sprayed with Pam and bake in a 350° oven until lightly browned on top.

NOTE: Can be refrigerated prior to baking if so will need to bake 45-60 minutes so that it heats through.

MEDIUM WHITE SAUCE
(USED IN CREAM CHICKEN RECIPE ON **PAGE 60**)

INGREDIENTS:

4 tablespoons butter
4 tablespoons flour
1 teaspoon salt
Dash of pepper
2 cups milk (whole or 2%)

Melt butter in double boiler or over VERY low heat.

Add flour, salt, and pepper, stir until well blended.

Remove from heat if in pan, (or remove top of double boiler) and gradually stir in milk.

Return to heat and cook, stirring constantly, until thick and smooth.

NOTE: Can be doubled.

EGGPLANT AND GROUND MEAT PARMIGIANA

(NANA CARMEN SYLVESTER)

INGREDIENTS:

eggplant (about 10" long)
ground meat (about 1 pound)
mozzarella cheese
grated parmesan/Romano cheese
flour
salt
black pepper
garlic (6-8 cloves)
milk
oil
seasoned bread crumbs
basil

Amount of ingredients depends on how much you want to make.

Prepare eggplant the day before by peeling outer skin and slicing into ¼"-½" thick slices. Place slices in large bowl sprinkling each layer with salt. Cover with plate and weigh down (you can use large can of vegetables on plate).

When ready to cook pour off liquid from eggplant. In a large bowl mix eggs, salt pepper, diced garlic, basil and cheese; let stand for 10 minutes.

In another bowl put in meat and salt to taste, pour in egg mixture add bread crumbs and mix. Mixture should be wet to the touch and soft, not firm like for meatballs.

Dredge eggplant in flour. In a large frying pan heat oil and cook a few slices of eggplant at a time, until lightly golden brown on each side. Remove to paper towel lined plate and drain. Repeat until all eggplant is fried. Use remaining oil to fry meat mixture which has been shaped into large flat patties (brown on both sides until firm but not hard). Remove meat to paper towel lined plate and drain. Repeat with additional meat until all meat is cooked.

In a flat baking dish layer spaghetti sauce, egg plant, meat (I usually slice meat patties to about 3/8" thickness), grated parmesan/romano cheese; repeat until all meat and egg plant used ending with spaghetti sauce, mozzarella and small amount of sauce. This may make more than one casserole.

Casserole may be frozen at this point or refrigerated. To cook bake in a 350° oven at least 45 minutes up to 1 hour 15 minutes.

NOTE: The more sauce the better. Sauce does not have to be very thick as it will cook into the eggplant and meat so can be thinned with water to extend it if needed.

MEATBALLS

(ITALIAN)

INGREDIENTS:

Ground beef

Seasoned bread crumbs

Oregano

Basil

Garlic powder

egg(s)

Grated parmesan cheese

Grated romano cheese

Amounts depend on how much meat you have. Mix all ingredients together to form a moist firm mixture. Form balls (I use and ice cream scoop to portion mixture then roll to smooth balls).

In a non-stick fry pan, brown meatballs on all sides; remove with slotted spoon to paper towel lined plate and drain. Once all are browned, place in pot of sauce and simmer 2 hours.

At this point you can serve over spaghetti or remove meatballs from sauce with slotted spoon and place on foil lined cookie sheet so that they do not touch and freeze overnight. The next day remove from cookie sheet and place in zip lock plastic bag, or bags, and return to freezer. This allows you to remove them as needed. Defrost and reheat in sauce to serve.

NOTE: Can be frozen without cooking in sauce, but will need to cook 2 hrs when removed from freezer.

SPAGHETTI SAUCE

INGREDIENTS:

1 green pepper
garlic cloves (10-12)
1 medium onion
olive oil
2 cans (6 ounces) tomato paste
basil
2 cans (28 ounces) tomato puree
oregano
2 cans (28 ounces) crushed tomatoes
garlic powder
onion powder
Italian spices (seasoning mix)

Dice onion, green pepper and 4-5 cloves garlic. In a 10-12" fry pan heat enough olive oil to just coat the bottom of the pan until it shimmers. Add diced vegetables and cook until onion is transparent and green pepper is soft.

In a large pot place canned tomato products, 5-6 cloves crushed garlic; add one can (from crushed tomatoes) full of water and mix. Sprinkle the surface with a layer of each; garlic powder, onion powder, basil, oregano and Italian spices; stir to mix. Add onion and green pepper, stir to mix.

Cook over low heat stirring occasionally 4-5 hours.

NOTE: Meatballs can be added after 3 hours if desired. Cool thoroughly and package for freezing if desired.

TUNA NOODLE CASSEROLE

INGREDIENTS:

8 ounce package Muller's Hearty noodles

1 can Campbell's cream of mushroom soup

1 can (6 ounces) tuna in water, well drained (or 1 large pouch Tuna in water)

Crispix or corn flakes crushed

Cook noodles per package directions and drain.

In pot you cooked noodles in, combine tuna and soup, mixing until smooth. Return noodles to pot and mix with soup mixture until noodles are well coated.

Place noodles in casserole dish that has been sprayed with vegetable oil spray. Crush crispix or corn flakes and sprinkle over top.

Bake in 350° for 30-45 minutes until top is lightly browned and crispy.

NOTE: doubles easily... reheats well.

MARA'S VARIATION

Add 1 small can evaporated milk and 1 generous cup shredded cheddar cheese to noodle/soup mixture and mix well before placing in casserole.

SWEET POTATO CASSEROLE

(PUDDING)

INGREDIENTS:

1 can (28 ounces size) sweet potatoes, drained
½ cup Crisco
½ cup dark Karo syrup
1 cup Rice Krispies
1 package miniature marshmallows

Beat together Crisco and sweet potatoes until light and fluffy. Add syrup and rice krispies while beating; continue until well mixed. Fold in 1-2 cups marshmallows.

Spoon into greased baking dish (10"x10", or 9"x13") and top with remaining marshmallows.

Bake at 350° for 45-60 minutes until marshmallows are melted and golden brown on top.

STUFFING

(THANKSGIVING)

INGREDIENTS:

1 16-ounce package Pepperidge Farms seasoned stuffing mix (not cube style)
1 cup diced fresh mushrooms
1 cup diced celery

Prepare stuffing per package directions adding mushrooms and celery along with liquid.

Place in greased casserole dish and bake at 325° 30-45 minutes.

SEASONING MIX

(MEAT AND POULTRY)

INGREDIENTS:

onion powder
garlic powder
paprika
(Use approximately the same size jar of each spice)

Pour each jar into a bowl and mix until well blended. Return mixture to jars and seal tightly to store.

MARINATED MUSHROOMS

(SERVED WITH STEAK)

INGREDIENTS:

1 large package fresh mushrooms
½ cup dry vermouth
½ cup dry sherry (I use Taylor's)
½ cup water
Lawry's seasoned pepper

Clean mushrooms and cut into halves or quarters depending on their size. Place in large bowl and set aside.

Put water, vermouth and sherry in 2 cup measure, sprinkle with seasoned pepper to taste and stir to mix.

Pour liquid over mushrooms and stir to coat; set aside or refrigerate until ready to cook. If mushrooms will sit more than 30 minutes, stir to recoat periodically.

Place mushrooms and LIQUID in fry pan and cook over medium heat until liquid has evaporated.

STUFFED CABBAGE

(SWEET AND SOUR)

INGREDIENTS:

1 head cabbage
1 large can tomatoes
1 pound ground beef
hot water
2 tablespoons brown sugar
1 teaspoon salt
½ cup raisins
½ teaspoon pepper
2 tablespoons raw (uncooked) rice
1 onion chopped fine
Lemon juice to taste (about 1 teaspoon)
1½ pounds short ribs

Separate leaves from cabbage, cutting away from core. Place in pot of boiling water and boil for a couple of minutes to wilt the cabbage. Remove from water and set aside to cool.

(If hard to separate leaves, place head under running HOT water with core toward faucet to soften and spread/separate leaves.)

Mix ground beef, salt, pepper, onion and rice; form into small balls (about golf ball size) and wrap in cabbage leaves using large leaves. Secure with toothpicks. Reserve small pieces to put in bottom of pot.

In large pot or Dutch oven braise short ribs. Place loose cabbage leaves on top of meat; place stuffed cabbage over this. Add tomatoes and hot water to cover. Add sugar, raisins and lemon juice to taste.

Bring to a boil, reduce heat and simmer covered for 2 hours adding more water if necessary to keep contents covered with liquid. Taste sauce and add more sugar or lemon juice as needed. Let simmer a few minutes longer.

CORN PUDDING

(SALLY STEWART)

INGREDIENTS:

1 can white cream style corn (14-3/4 oz)
1 can evaporated milk (5 fl oz size)
1 cup sugar
3 tablespoons corn starch
2 eggs
Butter or margarine

Put sugar and corn starch in a shallow 1½ quart baking dish and mix. Add eggs and mix well. Add corn and milk mix together. Dot top with butter.

Bake at 350° for 1 hour or until set. (Knife inserted in center comes out clean.)

VEGETABLE MARINADE

(FOR GRILLED VEGETABLES)

INGREDIENTS:
Vegetable oil (Crisco, etc)
Olive oil (slightly more than vegetable oil)
2 tablespoons water
5-6 drops Worcestershire sauce
1 tablespoon soy sauce
Fresh garlic (2-3 cloves)
Oregano

Combine all ingredients and mix well. Total amount should not exceed ½ cup. Pour over vegetables (mushrooms, peppers, squash, etc.) and toss to coat. Cook over grill.

MOM'S CUCUMBER SALAD

(A FAVORITE SOUTH AND NORTH)

INGREDIENTS:

**2 English (unpeeled) or regular (peeled)
cucumbers sliced thin**
1 onion sliced thin
1 teaspoon salt
1 cup distilled white vinegar
½ cup water
½ cup granulated sugar

Season cucumbers with salt in a large bowl and let sit 1 hour. Drain liquid and toss cucumbers with onion slices.

Put white vinegar and water in sauce pan and place over high heat. Stir in sugar until dissolved and liquid turns clear, 3-5 minutes.

Pour over cucumbers and onions. Cover with plastic wrap and regrigerate 1 hour. Serve cold or at room temperature.

NOTE: Tastes better the next day. Keeps refrigerated for up to three weeks.

BREAD AND BUTTER PICKLES

(ANDREA BUREAUX)

INGREDIENTS:

12 cups thinly sliced cucumbers
4 cups thinly sliced onions
2 green peppers diced
1 red pepper diced
6 cups sugar
2 teaspoons tumeric
2 teaspoons mustard seeds
4 cups vinegar
½ tsp celery seeds

Place cucumbers, onions, and peppers in large pot.

Dissolve ½ cup salt into water and pour over vegetables. Add enough water to cover the vegetables. Let stand at room temperature overnight.

Next morning pour off water and rinse thoroughly.

Mix sugar, tumeric, mustard seeds and celery seeds with vinegar. Pour over vegetables. Add more vinegar so you can see it in the pot.

Heat to boil and continue boiling for 5 minutes.

Place in clean glass jars while hot and seal with 2-piece lids. Jars should seal as they cool.

MARINADE FOR STEAK

(SETH BERKOWITZ)

INGREDIENTS:

1 part extra virgin olive oil
2 parts Worcestershire sauce
1 tablespoon (large splash) wine (any available)
Large splash either red wine or balsamic vinegar
¼ cup McCormick Montreal Steak Seasoning
Add Tobasco or other hot sauce for heat

NOTE: Adjust ingredients to taste at this point.

Combine all ingredients in a small bowl or 2 cup measuring cup and mix well.

Pierce meat and place in shallow pan or zip lock plastic bag. Pour marinade over meat. If in pan turn to coat, then cover with plastic wrap; in bag seal and turn to coat.

Let stand in refrigerator 4 hours or overnight.

CREAMED CHICKEN
(CHICKEN A LA KING)

INGREDIENTS:

4 tablespoons butter
4 tablespoons flour
1 teaspoon salt
Dash of pepper
2 cups milk (whole or 2%)
1 cup cubed cooked chicken

Melt butter in double boiler or over very low heat. Add flour, salt and pepper. Stir until well blended. Remove from heat (if in double boiler remove top pot from water) and gradually stir in milk. Return to heat. Cook, stirring constantly, until thick and smooth. Add chicken and stir to mix. Allow chicken to heat through before serving over toast.

Above recipe makes 2 cups. Can be made ahead and reheated.

NOTE: Recipe can be doubled or tripled easily. If doubling, increase salt by half; if tripling only double amount of salt.

GRAPE SALAD

INGREDIENTS:

1 pound seedless green grapes

8 ounces sour cream

1 pound seedless red grapes

½ cup granulated sugar

1 cup firmly packed brown sugar

1 tablespoon vanilla

¾ cup chopped pecans

1 8-ounce package cream cheese softened and at room temperature

Remove grapes from stems, wash and drain well; place in large serving bowl. Combine cream cheese and granulated sugar with hand mixer until smooth. Combine sour cream and vanilla in a separate bowl (or in the sour cream container—saves washing a bowl!).

Combine cream cheese and sour cream mixtures. Add to grapes stirring well. Top with brown sugar and pecans. Do not stir. Cover and chill overnight.

SHRIMP & GRITS

INGREDIENTS:

1 small Poblano pepper
½-¾ pounds tomatoes
1½ cup grits (cook per package directions using a combination of stock and milk, or all stock)*
2 tablespoons butter
Mascarpone or crème fraîche cheese (8 oz)
1 pound raw shrimp (peeled and deveined)
1 tablespoon chili oil
2 tablespoons vegetable oil
2 cloves garlic diced
t tablespoon fresh lemon juice
1 tablespoon grated lemon rind
¾ cup shredded cheddar cheese

Using a gas burner or grill, char Pablano and place in paper bag to sweat, then peel, remove seeds, and dice. Char tomatoes, slip off skin, and dice. (These 2 items are to taste and can be pureed together in a blender or folded into the grits.)

Marinate shrimp 30-45 minutes in oils, garlic, lemon juice, and grated lemon rind.

Cook grits.* When liquid absorbed mix in butter and crème fraîche or Mascarpone. Add shredded cheddar and mix well. Add the tomatoes and peppers (diced or pureed) and mix to blend.

Sautee shrimp in the marinade, turning a few times until pink (do not overcook!) I mix them into the grits leaving behind any marinade, however, they could be served on top of the grits with any residual marinade.

(A recipe exchange between professionals, I traded one of my recipes for this one from Harvest Moon Catering in Charlottesville, VA.)

Sweets
&
Desserts

BLUEBERRY TEA CAKE

INGREDIENTS:

2 cups sifted flour
2 teaspoons baking powder
½ teaspoon salt
¼ cup butter or margarine
¾ cup sugar
1 egg
½ cup milk (whole or 2%, NOT skim)
2 cups blueberries drained

Sift flour, baking powder and salt together. Cream butter and sugar, add egg and milk, and beat until smooth. Add dry ingredients, fold in blueberries.

Spread batter in 8 or 9" greased and floured pan. Sprinkle with crumb mixture (recipe below)*.

Bake in a preheated 375° oven 40 to 45 minutes.

*INGREDIENTS FOR CRUMB MIXTURE:

½ sugar
¼ cup flour
¾ teaspoon cinnamon
¼ cup butter or margarine

NOTE: (1) To keep blueberries from sinking to bottom of pan, toss with small amount of flour before adding to batter. (2) If desired can be baked as cupcakes or in mini-loaf pans which requires doubling the topping.

CHOCOLATE CAKE

INGREDIENTS:

2 sticks butter or margarine

2 cups sugar

2 eggs

4 squares unsweetened chocolate melted (1 oz each)

2½ cups flour

2 teaspoons baking soda

1 cup sour cream

1 cup boiling water

½ teaspoon salt

1 teaspoon vanilla

Cream butter and sugar together, add eggs and cream until light and fluffy. Add melted chocolate at lowest speed, mix until well blended. Add 1 ¼ cup flour, baking soda and salt and beat again. Add sour cream and mix. Add rest of flour and mix once more. After well blended add cup of water and vanilla and mix all through batter.

NOTE: Cake may look curdled —don't worry.

Pour into prepared pans and bake in a preheated 350° oven as follows:

In 3-8" round or square pans 30-35 minutes

In 2-9" pans for 40 minutes

In 1-9 x 13" pan for 40-45 minutes

MOTHER'S CHEESE CAKE

(JANE GABRIEL)

INGREDIENTS:

	Small	Large
Large curd cottage cheese	1 lb	1-1¼ lb
Cream cheese	¾ lb	1 lb
Juice and rind of orange	½ orange	1 orange
Eggs	4	6
Sour cream	1 scant cup	1¼ cups
Salt	½ teasp	½ teasp
Rounded tablespoons flour	6	9
Sugar	1 cup	1½ cups
Cherry pie filling	1 can	1-1½ cans

Small cake goes in either a spring form pan or two 9" round pans. Large cake goes in two 9" or 10" pans.

Make graham cracker crumb crust per directions on either box of crackers or package of crumbs. Mix crust in appropriate pan bringing 2/3's of way up sides.

Combine cottage cheese and orange juice in blender until creamy and smooth. Add cream cheese and blend again, add sour cream and blend. (If using a mixer combine in the same manner, beating after each until smooth and creamy, before adding the rest.)

Put above mixture in mixer bowl if in blender; add flour and salt and mix.

Put eggs in separate bowl and beat until light then gradually add sugar while beating until light, thick and creamy.

Gradually add eggs into cheese batter mixing at a *very low speed*. Batter will be very loose.

Pour into graham cracker crumb crust and bake in 325° oven for 1 hour in spring form pan or 45 minutes for other pans—until it feels almost firm in the middle when touched by finger.

Turn off oven, open door and let cake rest in oven for 1 hour. Remove and cool rest of way at room temperature. Top with pie filling (add red food coloring if desired to get deep red color).

NOTE: Cake will drop in the middle a little after it bakes or cools and may even crack.

CHOCOLATE ÉCLAIR CAKE

INGREDIENTS:

1 box graham crackers

2 small boxes Instant pudding mix (vanilla or French vanilla)

14 oz tub Cool Whip

3 cups milk

1 tub chocolate frosting

Mix pudding with 3 cups milk and let stand 5 minutes. Fold in Cool Whip.

Lightly grease bottom only of 11 x 13" glass baking pan. Cover bottom with layer of graham crackers. Put ½ pudding mixture on them; repeat graham crackers and pudding once more. Top with graham crackers and chocolate frosting.

. Cover with plastic wrap and chill over night.

DELICIOUS COFFEE CAKE

INGREDIENTS:

½ cup butter or margarine
1½ teaspoons baking powder
1 cup sugar
1 teaspoon vanilla
2 eggs
¼ cup sugar
1 cup sour cream
1 tablespoon cinnamon
1 teaspoon baking soda
2 tablespoons chopped nuts
1½ cup flour

Cream butter and **1 cup sugar,** add eggs; beat well. Add sour cream mixed with baking **soda** and flour sifted with baking **powder.** Add vanilla.

Turn half of batter into greased and floured 8 or 9" square pan or each of 2 9" round pans.

Mix ¼ cup sugar, cinnamon and nuts. Put about half of this mixture on top of batter and cover with remaining batter. Use remainder of mixture for topping on cake. (If using round pans use about half the mixture for each pan)

Bake in a 350° oven 45 minutes or until done; may take less time. Round pans take 30 minutes.

NOTE: Can be baked in a bundt pan. If using bundt pan place topping mixture in bottom of pan, half the batter, and rest of topping then batter instead of ending with topping.

HONEY CAKE

INGREDIENTS:

¾ **cup oil**
1 **teaspoon baking powder**
1 **cup sugar**
½ **teaspoon baking soda**
3 **eggs**
1 **teaspoon cinnamon**
4 **cups flour**
1 **teaspoon allspice**
1 **cup hot strong coffee**
½ **cup nuts**
½ **teaspoon salt**
½ **cup raisins**
1 **cup honey**

Sift together all dry ingredients EXCEPT baking soda.

Stir boiling hot coffee into ½ teaspoon baking soda and set aside.

Beat eggs together with oil, while continuing to beat, add sugar gradually. When well beaten add honey and beat well again.

While continuing to beat egg mixture alternately add flour and coffee mixtures ending with coffee. Add nuts and raisins. Pour into 2 greased 8 or 9" pans. Bake in a preheated 350° oven 1 hour or until tester comes out clean (check at 40 minutes).

PINEAPPLE CAKE

WITH CREAM CHEESE FROSTING*

INGREDIENTS:

2 cups sugar

1 cup crushed pineapple (8 oz can/do NOT drain)

2 cups flour

2 eggs

1 cup chopped nuts

2 teaspoons baking soda

1 teaspoon vanilla

Beat together **by hand** all ingredients. Pour into a greased and floured 9" x 13" pan. Bake in a preheated 350° oven 45 minutes. Frost while still warm with cream cheese frosting (recipe below).*

CREAM CHEESE FROSTING*

INGREDIENTS:

1 stick butter

1-1/3 cups powdered sugar

1 8-ounce cream cheese

1 teaspoon vanilla

Beat all ingredients together with mixer until smooth. Spread on warm cake and sprinkle with nuts.

NOTE: Cake freezes well and can be cut frozen to remove only that portion you desire.

DELICIOUS WHITE CAKE

INGREDIENTS:

Large cake	Small cake
2/3 cup shortening	½ cup shortening
(½ butter for flavor)	(½ butter for flavor)
1-¾ cups sugar	1-1/3 cups sugar
2-2/3 cups sifted flour	2 cups sifted flour
3½ teas baking powder	2½ teas baking powder
¾ teaspoon salt	½ teaspoon salt
1-1/3 cups thin milk	1 cup thin milk
(half water)	(half water)
2 teaspoons vanilla	1½ teaspoons vanilla
4 egg whites (½ cup)	3 egg whites (3/8 cup)
Stiffly beaten	Stiffly beaten
2-9" or 13"x9" pans	2-8" round or 1-9" square
greased and floured	greased and floured

Sift together flour, baking powder and salt. Cream together sugar and shortening until fluffy, alternately add flour mixture and milk mixed with vanilla, mixing well with each addition. Fold in egg whites. Pour into prepared pans. Bake in 350° oven until cake tests done.

Baking time: layers 30-35 minutes; square or oblong 35-45 minutes

NOTE: For cupcakes line muffin cups, fill 2/3 full, bake at 400° for 18-20 minutes. Small cake makes 14; large makes about 20 cupcakes.

SCHNECKEN

INGREDIENTS:

½ **pound butter**

1 cake yeast or 1 pkg dry yeast

1 scant cup sugar

2 eggs

1 heaping teaspoon salt

about 6 cups flour

1 cup boiling water

1 cup cold water

Add butter to water and stir until melted, then cool. Break eggs into bowl; add sugar and salt. Add cold water to butter and boiling water mixture; pour into egg mixture; crumble in yeast cake or sprinkle dry yeast over top. Add flour and knead into ball. Cover and put in refrigerator for 24 hours.

Following day, roll out to preferred shapes. Place in muffing tins which have brown sugar, butter and pecans in bottom. (Or make twists, brush with melted butter: add raisins, currants, cinnamon and brown sugar.) Cover and let rise 2 to 3 hours.

Bake at 350° 20-30 minutes. Remove from muffin pans and cool on wire rack.

RICH YELLOW CAKE
(BIRTHDAY)

INGREDIENTS:

Large cake	*Small cake*
2/3 cup shortening	½ cup shortening
(½ butter for flavor)	(½ butter for flavor)
1½ cups sugar	1-1/8 cup sugar
3 eggs (1/2 to2/3 cup)	2 eggs (1/3 to ½ cup)
2¼ cups sifted flour	1¾ cups sifted flour
2½ tsp baking powder	2 tsp baking powder
1 teaspoon salt	¾ teaspoons salt
1 cup milk	¾ cup milk
1½ teaspoons vanilla	1 teaspoon vanilla
2-9" layer pans or	2-8" round layer pans or
13" x 9" oblong	1-9" square pan

Grease and flour pans.

Cream together shortening and sugar until fluffy. Beat eggs in until thoroughly blended. Sift together flour, baking powder and salt. Mix vanilla into milk.

Alternately add flour mixture and milk to eggs and shortening while continuing to beat at low speed until well blended.

Pour into prepared pans and bake in a preheated 350° oven: Layers 25-30 minutes, square or oblong 30-40 minutes.

NOTE: For cupcakes line muffin cups, fill 2/3 full, bake at 400° for 18-20 minutes. Small cake makes 14; large makes about 20 cupcakes.

FUDGE BROWNIES

(MARA NEBOSHYNSKY)

INGREDIENTS:

½ **cup margarine**

2 eggs

1 cup sugar

½ **cup flour**

2 1-ounce squares of unsweetened chocolate

1 teaspoon vanilla

On low heat melt margarine and chocolate. Remove from heat and stir in sugar. Add eggs; stir until you do not see any streaks of egg. Stir in flour and vanilla.

Spray 8" square pan with Pam; spoon batter into pan.

Bake in a 350° oven 30-35 minutes.

DECORATOR'S FROSTING

INGREDIENTS:

1 pound confectioner's sugar
½ cup (level) Crisco
¼ teaspoon salt
¼ cup water
1 teaspoon vanilla (white)

With electric mixer, beat Crisco until creamy: about 2 minutes.

Turn off mixer and dump in sugar, sprinkle salt around and add rest of ingredients; beat at higher speed 3-5 minutes until light and creamy.

If too dry, add water a drop at a time.

If frosting is too sweet, use 2 tablespoons flour when mixing.

Store in a tightly sealed container at room temperature.

Single batch will frost and decorate oblong cake. To frost and decorated layer cake make a double batch.

NOTE: If you use dark vanilla, frosting will appear cream rather than pure white.

DECORATOR'S FUDGE FROSTING

INGREDIENTS:

¼ **cup Crisco melted**

½ **cup cocoa**

¼ **teaspoon salt**

1/3 cup milk

1 teaspoon vanilla

1 pound confectioner's sugar

Melt Crisco add cocoa and mix well. Add salt, milk, and vanilla. Mix well again. Put confectioner's sugar in a bowl, add the chocolate mixture and beat until smooth. It will be thick. Add a tiny bit of milk to thin down if necessary to achieve a spreadable consistency.

CHOCOLATE CHIP COOKIES

INGREDIENTS:

2¼ cups flour
¾ cup granulated sugar
1 teaspoon baking soda
¾ cup packed brown sugar
1 teaspoon salt
1 teaspoon vanilla extract
1 cup (2 sticks) butter, softened
2 eggs
1 cup chopped nuts (optional)
1¾ cups (11.5 ounce package) chocolate morsels

Sift together baking soda, flour and salt, set aside. Beat with mixer butter, sugars and vanilla until light and creamy, add eggs and beat again. Gradually beat in flour mixture. Stir in chocolate morsels and nuts (if using).

Drop by rounded tablespoon onto ungreased baking sheets. Bake in in a preheated 375° oven 9 to 11 minutes or until golden brown Cool on wire racks.

COOKIE PRESS COOKIES

INGREDIENTS:

2¼ cups flour
1 cup shortening
¾ cup sugar
1 egg
¼ teaspoon baking powder
1 teaspoon vanilla
½ teaspoon salt

Sift flour, sugar, baking powder and salt together in a bowl. With pastry blender or two knives cut the shortening into the dry ingredients until the mixture is full of fine lumps. It will resemble pie crust or biscuit mix, although not as coarse.

Measure the egg in a measuring cup. A large egg will measure ¼ cup. If it does not, add water to the ¼ cup line.

Add the egg and vanilla and beat the mixture very well. Add food coloring as desired.

Put through cookie press onto ungreased cookie sheets. Bake in a preheated 375° oven 10-12 minutes. Remove to cooling rack and cool.

NOTE: Do NOT double recipe as mixer can't handle it.

ANGIE'S BISCOTTI

(ANGIE MARTELLA)

INGREDIENTS:

1 pound flour
1 pound sugar
8 ounces almonds
5 large eggs

Mix flour, sugar and nuts together in bowl. Make a well and put eggs in well. Beat together all ingredients until blended.

Spray a cookie sheet with Pam. Divide dough into 2 parts. Place both on cookie sheet, shape each to resemble a bread strip.

Bake in a preheated 350° oven 15-20 minutes until just starting to brown. REMOVE from pan and cut into 1" thick slices. Place slices back on cookie sheet cut side up. RETURN to oven and continue baking until golden brown

GINGER SNAPS

INGREDIENTS:

	Single	*Double*
Shortening	¾ cup	1½ cups
Packed brown sugar	1 cup	2 cups
Egg(s)	1	2
Molasses	¼ cup	½ cup
Flour	2¼ cups	4½ cups
Baking soda	2 tsps	4 tsps
Salt	¼ tsp	½ tsp
Ground cloves	½ tsp	1 tsp
Cinnamon	1 tsp	2 tsps
Ginger	1 tsp	2 tsps

Mix together first 4 ingredients and set aside. Sift together dry ingredients and stir into egg mixture.

Refrigerate dough for 15-30 minutes or until set. Roll into balls the size of walnuts, and dip tops in sugar.

Place on greased cookie sheet 3" apart.

Bake in preheated 375° oven 10-12 minutes until set but not hard.

HALF MOON COOKIES

(AUNT IDA YOUNGERMAN)

INGREDIENTS:

1 cup margarine
1½ teaspoons baking powder
½ cup sugar
1 teaspoon baking soda
2 eggs
1 cup sour milk *
3½ cups flour
1 teaspoon vanilla

Combine shortening and sugar until creamy; add eggs and rest of ingredients ending with flour.

Drop by soupspoon-full onto ungreased cookie sheet.

Bake in preheated 350° oven 10-15 minutes. Cool on wire rack. When thoroughly cooled, frost half of each cookie with chocolate frosting and half with white frosting to form half moon pattern.

*NOTE: To make sour milk add 1 tablespoon vinegar to 1 cup milk

MOLASSES RAISIN COOKIES

INGREDIENTS:

½ **cup shortening (or margerine)**
1 **cup sugar**
1 **egg**
3 **cups sifted flour**
1 **teaspoon baking soda**
1 **teaspoon salt**
1 **teaspoon ginger**
1 **teaspoon cinnamon**
1 **teaspoon baking soda**
¾ **cup undiluted evaporated milk**
¾ **teaspoons vinegar**
½ **cup molasses**
1 **cup raisins**

Sift together flour, baking soda, salt, ginger and cinnamon; set aside.

Beat together shortening, sugar and egg.

To evaporated milk, add vinegar then molasses; stir to mix. Combine with shortening mixture mixing well.

Slowly add liquid/shortening mixture to flour mixture beating at low speed with mixer until well blended. Add raisins and mix to blend.

Drop on greased cookie sheet and bake 15 minutes in a 350° oven.

REFRIGERATOR COOKIES

INGREDIENTS:

1 cup shortening
1 cup confectioner's sugar
2¾ cups flour
1 teaspoon vanilla
2 or 3 tablespoons milk

Combine ingredients to form a thick batter. Shape into 2 rolls approximately 2" in diameter. Wrap each in wax paper and refrigerate at least 3 hours or overnight.

Cut into 1/8" slices and place on ungreased cookie sheet.

Bake in a preheated 400° oven 8-10 minutes until lightly brown.

NOTE: Dough may be tinted with food coloring before shaping into roll or cookies may be sprinkled with colored sugar before baking if desired.

NEVER FAIL STRUDEL

INGREDIENTS:

¾ **cup oil (canola or vegetable)**
½ **teaspoon salt**
1 cup granulated sugar
2 teaspoons baking powder
2 eggs
2 teaspoons vanilla
½ **cup orange juice or water**
4 to 4½ cups flour

    Mix ingredients as listed until consistency to roll. **DO NOT USE ELECTRIC MIXER.** Divide into 3 or 4 parts, rolling each until ¼ inch thick. Spread with prune butter or jelly, sprinkle with cinnamon – sugar, raisins, chopped nuts, coconut if desired, leaving a ½ inch border on 1 long and both short sides. Roll like jelly roll starting at unboardered edge. Transfer carefully to cookie sheet; sprinkle with cinnamon-sugar.

    Bake in 350° oven 30-45 minutes until golden brown. Cool 10 minutes on cookie sheet; transfer to wire rack to complete cooling.

RUGELACH

(PARVE)

INGREDIENTS:

3 eggs
1 teaspoon baking powder
¾ cup oil
1 teaspoon lemon juice
1 cup sugar
2 tablespoons water
2 or more cups flour

Mix ingredients (best if done by hand) adding flour until it no longer sticks to finger and is right consistency to roll with rolling pin. Roll out 1/8" thick; cut into 4 inch squares.

Spread with jam or jelly or place your favorite filling (raisins, chopped dates, nuts, cinnamon and sugar, brown sugar) in one corner of each square and roll up.

Place on cookie sheet and bake in 350° oven 15-20 minutes or until lightly browned.

RUGELACH DOUGH

(DAIRY)

INGREDIENTS:

1 cup flour, sifted
¼ teaspoon salt
¼ pound butter
¼ pound cream cheese

Sift flour and salt into a bowl. Mix in other ingredients by hand. Roll out on lightly floured board. Fold dough over three times, wrap, and chill overnight.

Next day roll out to 1/8" thickness, cut into 4 inch squares. Spread with jam, jelly or place your favorite filling (raisins, chopped dates, nuts, cinnamon and sugar, brown sugar) in one corner of each square and roll up.

Place on cookie sheet and bake in 350° oven 15-20 minutes or until lightly browned.

STRAWBERRY PIE

INGREDIENTS:

1 9" baked pie shell
1-1½ quarts fresh berries
1 cup sugar
¼ teaspoon salt
½ cup water
1½ tablespoons cornstarch
2 teaspoons lemon juice

Combine 1 cup berries, salt, sugar and ¼ cup water in blender and pulse to crush berries; pour into sauce pan. Stir cornstarch with ¼ cup water and add to sauce pan. Cook over medium heat stirring constantly until thick and clear. Cool about 5 minutes and stir in lemon juice.

Fill shell with remaining berries, pour thickened mixture over. Let set 5 hours or over night. Top with whipped topping if desired before serving.

PUMPKIN PIE

INGREDIENTS:

1 unbaked 9" (4 cup volume) pie shell
¾ cup granulated sugar
½ teaspoon ground ginger
½ teaspoon salt
¼ teaspoon ground cloves
1 teaspoon ground cinnamon
2 eggs
1¾ cups (15 ounce can) Libby's solid pack
  pumpkin
1½ cups (12 fluid ounce can) evaporated milk

Combine sugar, salt, cinnamon, ginger, and cloves in a small bowl. Beat eggs lightly in large bowl. Stir in pumpkin and sugar mixture. Gradually stir in evaporated milk. Pour into pie shell.

Bake for 15 minutes in a preheated 425° oven. Reduce temperature to 350° bake for 40-50 minutes or until knife inserted near center comes out clean.

NOTE: You can use Libby's canned pumpkin pie and follow the directions on the can. (Eliminates the need for spices listed above.)

RICE PUDDING

INGREDIENTS:

2/3 cup cooked rice

1 quart milk

1 large can evaporated milk (12 oz size)

2/3 cup sugar

2 tablespoons corn starch

2 eggs beaten

1 teaspoon vanilla

1 cup raisins

In a 3 quart sauce pan bring milk and evaporated milk to simmer. Add rice, sugar, eggs and cornstarch. Heat to boil and cook 2 minutes. Add vanilla and raisins.

Spoon into individual serving dishes and cool.

NOTE: Will be thin until thoroughly cooled. Do NOT use fast cook rice.

CHOCOHOLIC'S
DUTCH COCOA MIX

INGREDIENTS:

1 cup granulated sugar

1 ½ teaspoons vanilla extract

1 cup Dutch process coca (Droste, Van Houten, etc)

¾ cup nondairy creamer (Creamora or Coffee Mate, not light)

3/8 teaspoon salt

3 cups nonfat dry milk

Put sugar into an ovenproof dish, add the vanilla and mix well. Dry this mixture in a 250° oven until all moisture is gone—it will get lumpy and crusty.

Put other ingredients into the bowl of a food processor fitted with the steel blade. Process mixture until powdery and completely mixed. Add sugar mixture and mix well again—about 1 minute. This will help it dissolve in water.

Put into an airtight container—a one pound coffee can is the right size.

KENTUCKY BOURBON BALLS

INGREDIENTS:

1 pound powdered sugar
1 stick butter (or margarine) softened
4 tablespoons Bourbon (I use Woodford Reserve)
 or any other spirit

Mix together by hand until well mixed and you can form a large ball.

Wrap in plastic wrap or put in airtight container and chill for at least 1 hour.

Pinch off about 2 teaspoons of the mixture and roll into a ball; place on waxed paper covered cookie sheet. Should make 30-32 balls

Chill in fridge or freezer until firm. The colder they are the better they hold up when dipped in chocolate. (Recipe next page.)

1 pound powdered sugr

DIPPING CHOCOLATE

INSTRUCTIONS:

2 8-oz bars Bakers German Sweet Chocolate, chopped
1/8 of a paraffin bar finely chopped (or grated with a vegetable grater). The paraffin melts slower than the chocolate, so finer/smaller is better.

NOTE: You can also use chocolate chips, candy melt coating, or white chocolate.

Melt chocolate and paraffin in a double boiler over very low heat, or set a bowl in a larger bowl or pan of boiling water. Stir until melted and smooth. Be careful not to get any water in the chocolate!!

Using a fork or toothpicks, dip balls 1 at a time in melted chocolate and set on waxed paper covered tray. Chill until cocolate is set.

Store balls in an airtight container with waxed paper between layers. They keep for a long time if you can keep everybody out of them.

NOTE: Leftover chocolate can be saved and re-melted for later use.

BUCKEYES

(LEAH BUSSE)

INGREDIENTS:

1 pound margarine
2 pounds smooth peanut butter
3 pounds confectioners sugar

In a large bowl combine all ingredients until smooth. Roll into small balls, about 1/4 inch.

Place in refrigerator for about 20 minutes before coating with chocolate.

DIPPING CHOCOLATE INGREDIENTS:

1 pound Hershey bar, grated
1 pound semi-sweet chocolate chips
1-1/3 to 3 ounces of grated paraffin

In a double boiler or an electric fondue pot melt all ingredients.

Using toothpicks or fork, dip peant butter balls in chocolate, one at a time.

Placed on waxed paper covered cookie sheet and refrigerate until set.

Store in an airtight container in cool place or refrigerator.

NOTE: Place layer of waxed paper between layers of balls and over the top layer before sealing the container.

LEMON-BLUEBERRY DUTCH BABY

(BOB TETRAULT)

INGREDIENTS:

1 cup milk

¾ cup flour

2 tablespoons granulated sugar

4 large eggs

Zest of 1 lemon

½ teaspoon salt

4 tablespoons butter

¾ cup fresh blueberries

2 tablespoons powdered sugar

1 teaspoon vanilla extract

Place rack in middle of oven. Preheat to 425°

In a blender combine milk, flour, sugar, salt, eggs, lemon zest, and vanilla and blend until smooth.

Place butter in a heavy ovenproof 10-12 inch skillet (such as cast iron). Place in hot oven for 3-5 minutes or until butter is melted. Remove from oven and swirl pan to coat with melted butter. Pour batter into pan and add blueberries.

Bake 17-20 minutes or until puffed and golden. Remove pan from oven and sprinkle with powdered sugar.

Serve with lemon curd (available in grocery stores).

Serves 4-6.

CHOCOLATE CHERRY HEART SMART COOKIES

(ALLIS HANLEY)

INGREDIENTS:

1/3 cup white flour
1/3 cup whole wheat flour
1½ cup rolled oats
1 teaspoon baking soda
¾ cup packed light brown sugar
1 cup dried cherries
1 teaspoon vanilla
1 large egg, lightly beaten
2 ounces coarsely chopped bittersweet chocolate chunks

Preheat oven to 325 °

Lightly mix both flours, oats, baking soda, and salt in a large bowl.

Melt butter over low heat, add brown sugar, and stir until smooth.

Add dry ingredients and beat with mixer until well blended.

Add cherries, vanilla, and egg. Fold in chocolate chunks

Place dough by spoonful onto baking sheet coated in cooking spray.

Bake for 12 minutes.

BROYE DU POITOU

(JACQUELINE LAWSON)

INGREDIENTS:

1 egg

8 ounces flour (Use kitchen scale to measure*)

4 ounces sugar (Use kitchen scale to measure*)

4 ounces butter (Use kitchen scale to measure*)

A pinch of salt

A teaspoon of cognac (Optional)

An egg yolk (for glazing)

Sift flour and set aside.

Mix the egg with the sugar and salt; optionally add cognac. Gradually add the butter, cut into small pieces. Add the flour and mix to form a ball. Try not to overwork the mixture. Wrap the ball of pastry in plastic wrap and put in fridge for an hour. Meanwhile heat the oven to 350°.

Roll pastry into a large circle about 1/2-inch thick and place on cookie sheet. Form a petal pattern around the edge by pinching with your fingers; then glaze the biscuit with egg yolk. Finally: make a decorative grid across the biscuit with a fork and scatter almonds on top.

Bake the biscuit in the oven for about 25 minutes. When cold, break into pieces by thumping it in the middle with your fist.

*NOTE: Europeans measure dry and solid ingredients by weight on a scale rather than using measuring cups.

BLUEBERRY COBBLER

(FROM CHESTERFIELD BERRY FARM)

INGREDIENTS FOR FILLING:

1 stick butter
1 teaspoon lemon juice
4 cups fresh blueberries, rinsed and drained
1 cup sugar

INGREDIENTS FOR TOPPING:

1 cup self-rising flour*
1 cup sugar
1 teaspoon vanilla
½ cup milk

Preheat oven to 375°.

Place the butter in an 8"x8" square glass baking dish (no substitutes) and melt butter in microwave.

In a mixing bowl, combine lemon juice and blueberries. Add the sugar and mix well. Add the blueberry mixture to the baking dish with the melted butter. DO NOT STIR.

Make the topping by combining all ingredients in a small bowl. Pour this mixture over the blueberries and bake for 45 minutes or until golden brown.

*NOTE: Make your own self-rising flour: Mix 1 cup flour and 1½ teaspoons baking POWDER and ½ teaspoon salt.

Serve with optional whipped cream or vanilla ice cream.

BLACKBERRY COBBLER

(FROM CHESTERFIELD BERRY FARM)

INGREDIENTS:

1 quart blackberries
2 cups sugar divided
1 stick margarine
1 cup milk
1 cup self-rising flour*

Preheat oven to 450°.

In a saucepan over medium heat bring blackberries, 1 cup sugar, and enough water to make blackberries juicy, to a boil and cook for 10 minutes.

Melt margarine in a 9"x13" baking dish in the oven until margarine is lightly browned. Remove from oven.

Combine milk, sugar and flour, beating hard until lumps are gone. Pour batter over melted margarine. Bake 5-10 minutes. Pour berries over the batter and bake an additional 10-15 minutes or until cobbler is browned.

*NOTE: Make your own self-rising flour: Mix 1 cup flour and 1-1/2 teaspoons baking POWDER and 1/2 teaspoon salt.

RED VELVET LAYER CAKE

AND

CREAM CHEESE FROSTING

INGREDIENTS FOR CAKE:

1 cup butter, softened
2½ cups sugar
6 large eggs
3 cups all-purpose flour
3 tablespoons unsweetened cocoa
¼ teaspoon baking SODA
1 8-oz container sour cream
2 teaspoons vanilla extract
2 1-oz bottles red food coloring

Preheat oven to 350°.

Beat butter at medium speed with a stand mixer until creamy.

Gradually add sugar, beating until light and fluffy.

Add eggs, 1 at a time, beating just until blended after each addition.

Sift together flour, cocoa, and baking soda. Add to butter mixture alternately with sour cream, beginning and ending with the flour mixture. Beat at low speed until just blended after each addition.

Stir in vanilla. Stir in red food coloring.

Spoon cake batter into 3 greased and floured 8-inch round cake pans.

Bake at 350° for 18-20 minutes, or until a wooden pick inserted into the center comes out clean. Cool in pans on wire rack 10 minutes. Remove from pans to wire racks and let cool 1 hour, or until completely cool.

INGREDIENTS FOR CREAM CHEESE FROSTING:

2 8-oz packages (brick style) cream cheese, softened

½ cup butter, softened

1 pound powderd sugar

2 teaspoons vanilla extract

Beat cream cheese and butter at medium speed with an electric mixer until creamy. Gradually add powdered sugar, beating until fluffy. Stir in vanilla.

Assemble cake by placing 1 layer on a plate or serving platter, spread frosting on top, place next layer on this and spread with frosting, place final layer on top.

Frost sides of cake and then the top.

JEWISH APPLE CAKE

(ALLIS HANLEY)

Preheat oven to 350°
Grease and flour angel food pan (set aside)

Mix together:

4 large apples (6 cups) peeled, cored and sliced
5 tablespoons sugar
2 teaspoons cinnamon
Set aside until later

Next mix:

3 cups UNSIFTED flour
2 cups sugar
3 level teaspoons baking POWDER
½ teaspoon salt
4 eggs
1 cup salad oil (such as Crisco or Wesson)
1/3 cup orange juice
2½ teaspoons vanilla

Using an electric mixer combine the above and beat 3-4 minutes at a medium speed.

Put half the batter in the pan. Add half the apple mixture on top, then the rest of the batter and finish with the remaining apple mixture.

Bake 1-3/4 to 2 hours until a cake tester comes out dry. When cake is done, cool in pan for about 20 minutes. Turn cake out of pan, and then turn over so apples are on top. Allow to cool completely.

5-MINUTE CHOCOLATE BUTTER CREAM FROSTING

INGREDIENTS:

6 tablespoons UNSALTED butter
2-1/3 cups confectioners sugar
¾ cup unsweetened cocoa powder
1/3 cup milk
1 teaspoon vanilla
¼ teaspoon salt

In bowl of stand mixer fitted with paddle attachment, beat the butter on medium speed until smooth, about 1 minute.

Add the confectioners sugar and cocoa and beat until combined. With mixer on low speed, slowly stream in the milk and vanilla, then add the salt. Continue beating until well combined, scraping down the sides as needed, about 2 minutes. Increase the speed to high and beat for an additional 2 minutes.

Use frosting immediately or store in an airtight container in the fridge. If you refrigerate the frosting you may want to allow it to come to room temperature and re-blend in the mixer for a few seconds before using.

NOTES

"When you dine at Devra's table you are home with family. Master chef with Mother's love blended into every bite."
—Richard & Bette Meade
(New York)

Jewish Holiday

CARROT TZIMMES

(HIGH HOLIDAY CASSAROLE)

INGREDIENTS:

1½-2 pounds carrots
1 teaspoon salt
4 pounds beef brisket
½ cup brown sugar

Put brisket in LARGE pot (one that can also go in the oven), cover with water and put on to cook, add salt. (Cook over medium heat.)

Scrape and slice carrots. After meat has cooked 1 hour add carrots, spreading around meat; continue cooking until meat is almost tender (about another hour). Add brown sugar to pot then make Knoedle (recipe below).

Drop Knoedle into carrots around meat, baste with liquid, cover and cook 30 minutes.

Uncover and place in preheated 350° oven. Bake until Knoedle is golden brown.

KNOEDLE

(DUMPLING)

INGREDIENTS:

3 cups flour
2 eggs
1 small onion, grated
½ teaspoon salt
1 tablespoon sugar
3 tablespoons oil
about 2 cups water

Put flour, eggs, grated onion, salt, sugar and oil in large bowl. Beat in one cup water mixing well; add enough more water to make a thick running batter.

AUNT IDA'S TAIGLACH

(HONEY CANDY-SOFT)

INGREDIENTS:

4 eggs
1½ pounds honey
pinch of salt
1 teaspoon whiskey
½ cup water
¾ cup sugar
1¾ - 2 cups flour
½ teaspoon ginger

Beat eggs until light; add salt and whiskey. Continue beating with a fork while adding flour a little at a time. Dough should be soft and when pulled with a fork you get a large piece. Let rest in bowl 5 minutes.

Flour board and hands; take a little dough and roll into a long rope ½" - ¾" in diameter, cut into ½" pieces. Repeat until all dough has been used. Let rest on board 1 hour.

In a large, deep pot place honey, sugar, water and ginger. Bring to a full boil. Using knife add dough to pot, cover tightly, reduce heat (to low flame) and cook 30 minutes **without looking.** After 30 minutes look to be sure it isn't burning, re-cover and boil another 10 minutes stirring once or twice during this time, check again. Continue cooking for 10 minute intervals until golden brown.

Remove from heat and pour ¾ cup boiling water over taigle. Using a slotted spoon remove from pot and store in containers.

GRANDMA JANE'S TAIGLACH

(HONEY CANDY-LIKE NUT BRITTLE)

INGREDIENTS:

2 cups sifted flour
1/8 teaspoon salt
1 teaspoon baking powder
3 eggs
3 tablespoons oil
1 pound honey
1½ cups sugar
1 teaspoon ginger
1 cup filbert nuts

Sift flour, salt and baking powder into a bowl, add eggs and oil, beat with a fork at first then knead until all flour is mixed in forming a dough ball. Break off pieces and roll into pencil thin strips, cut strips into ½ " pieces. Repeat until all dough is used.

Put honey and sugar in a large deep pot and bring to a rolling boil. Add dough pieces spreading around in honey so pieces do not stick together. Cover pot. Do **not stir** for 20 minutes. Shake pot occasionally to prevent burning at bottom. Uncover pot and cook for another 5-10 minutes testing honey in cold water. When a soft ball forms remove from heat.

Add ginger and nuts, stir well. Spread on cutting board and flatten with moistened hands.

After it becomes cool and sticky cut with a sharp knife cut in diamond or square pieces.

If desired sprinkle with additional ginger. Allow to cool completely and store in airtight containers.

LUCKSHION KUGEL

(NOODLES)

INGREDIENTS:

1 pound broad noodles
¼ cup butter or margarine
2-4 tablespoons sugar
1 pint sour cream
1 pound cottage cheese
4 eggs
cinnamon and raisins (to your taste)

Cook noodles as directed, drain and rinse with hot water. Return to pot, cut margarine into chunks, and add to hot noodles mixing until well covered.

In large mixing bowl or blender combine eggs, sour cream, cottage cheese and sugar until smooth.

Fold egg mixture into noodles.

Pour half of the noodle mixture into a well greased 9" x 13" baking pan; sprinkle liberally with cinnamon and raisins. Cover with rest of noodles and marble. Sprinkle top with cinnamon and sugar.

Using a spatula, drag through pan in a figure eight to marble cinnamon into noodles. If any raisins are exposed on top, push them down so they are covered to prevent them from burning.

Bake in a 350° oven 1½ hours.

NOTE: can be baked in 2 9" square pans –reduce cooking time to 45 minutes. Can be frozen either before or after baking.

BLINTZ SOUFFLE

(USING CREPES)

INGREDIENTS:

4 eggs
4 tablespoons sugar
1 pint sour cream
1 teaspoon vanilla
12 cheese blintzes (store bought or homemade)

Combine eggs, sour cream, sugar and vanilla in blender until smooth, creamy and well mixed.

In a well greased shallow baking dish place blintzes in single layer, pour sour cream mixture over them.

Bake in a preheated 325° oven until golden brown (about 1 hour).

CHEESE BLINTZES

(CREPES)

INGREDIENTS:

4 eggs

¾ cup flour

½ teaspoon salt

1 teaspoon sugar

1 pound cottage cheese or ½ pound each farmer and cottage cheese

For blintz (crepe) combine 3 eggs, flour and salt to form a thin batter. Heat and 6" skillet and grease: pour small amount of batter in pan tipping to thinly coat bottom. Cook until edges start to separated from pan, turn out onto waxed paper. Repeat with rest of batter.

Combine cheese, 1 egg and sugar to form filling. Drop by tablespoons in center of each blintz, fold edges over filling to form sealed envelope. Repeat procedure until all filling and blintzes are used.

Cook by frying in butter until brown on both sides or bake in a 350° oven until brown. Serve with sour cream or cinnamon sugar.

NOTE: Before cooking blintzes can be frozen or used in blintz souffle recipes.

POTATO KUGEL

(PIE OR CASSEROLE)

INGREDIENTS:

6 potatoes
3 tablespoons oil
1 onion
3 tablespoons flour
1 teaspoon baking powder
2 eggs
salt and pepper to taste

Grate potatoes on fine grater or in blender. (If using blender, add onions to last batch of potato to be grated.) Remove excess water. Add finely grated onion and other ingredients. Grease well a 10" glass pie pan or suitable baking dish, pour in kugel.

Bake in a 350° oven 1½ hours or until golden brown.

NOTE: For individual kugels place mixture in well greased muffin tin(s) and bake at 350° for 1 hour.

To use blender, grate in batches, draining excess water after grating. After first batch reserve water to use in next batch. Repeat until all potatoes are grated.

POTATO LATKES
(HANNUKAH POTATO PANCAKES)

INGREDIENTS:

2 cups grated raw potatoes (about 4 or 5)
1 medium onion grated (optional)
2 eggs, well beaten
1 teaspoon salt
Dash of pepper
1 tablespoon flour
Oil for frying

Peel potatoes and grate; drain off water. Add eggs, salt, pepper, and flour mixing thoroughly. Heat oil (almost deep enough to cover the pancakes) and drop batter by tablespoon into hot oil. Fry over moderate heat until brown and crisp around the edges; turn and brown other side. Drain on paper towels. Serves 4-5.

Serve with sugar, cinnamon and sugar mix, applesauce, sour cream, or honey,

PASSOVER SPONGE CAKE

INGREDIENTS:

9 eggs (at room temperature)
1½ cups sugar
¾ cup potato starch
1 lemon
¼ cup (rounded) cake meal
Dash of salt

Separate eggs placing whites in large bowl and yolks in smaller bowl. Add salt to egg whites and beat until stiff; slowly add the sugar while beating until all sugar is dissolved. Grate whole lemon, remove any pits. Beat the yolks until thick and light; add grated lemon and mix well. Pour yolk mixture over the whites and gently fold in by hand.

Sift together cake meal and potato starch; gradually fold into eggs being certain that no flour remains on bottom of bowl. (Fold by hand do NOT use mixer) Pour into **ungreased** 9" or 10" tubular pan.

Bake in a **300°** oven 1-1¼ hours until done. Remove from oven, invert pan on rack or over neck of glass bottle and cool thoroughly before removing from pan.

NOTE: To remove from pan, run a sharp knife around the outer edge of the cake inside the pan and lift out the center of the pan. Run knife around center of the cake near edge of the tube and under cake against bottom of pan.

NOTES

"My mother was a great cook and baker. Devra is her equal."
—Charles Holt, VA

Baby
& Kids

BABY'S HEALTH CRACKERS*

INGREDIENTS:

2½ cups sifted whole wheat flour
2 tablespoons soy flour
2 teaspoons wheat germ
2 tablespoons nonfat dry milk powder
3 tablespoons oil
3 tablespoons honey
1 teaspoon vanilla
2/3 cup milk

Mix together whole wheat and soy flours, nonfat dry milk powder and wheat germ. Combine oil, honey, and vanilla. Blend the liquid ingredients with the dry ingredients. Knead until they form a smooth ball. Roll on floured sheet until as thin as possible. Cut into 1 inch strips.

Bake at 350° on greased cookie sheet for 8-10 minutes until brown.

Remove from cookie sheet, cool thoroughly on cooling racks and store in tightly covered container.

*NOTE: Not for children younger than 1 year; contains honey.

TEETHING BISCUITS
(CRISP)

INGREDIENTS:

1 beaten egg yolk
2 tablespoons honey
2 tablespoons molasses
2 tablespoons oil
1 teaspoon vanilla
¾ cup whole wheat flour
1 tablespoon soy flour
1 tablespoon wheat germ
1½ tablespoons nonfat dry milk powder

Mix together whole wheat and soy flours, wheat germ and nonfat dry milk, set aside. Blend egg yolk, honey, molasses, oil and vanilla, add dry mixture. Roll out dough very thin (1/8-1/4" thick). Cut in baby finger length rectangles.

Bake at 350° on ungreased cookie sheet for 15 minutes.

Remove from cookie sheet, and cool thoroughly on cooling racks and store in tightly covered container.

NOTE: Not for children younger than 1 year; contains honey.

HOMEMADE PLAY DOUGH

INGREDIENTS:

3 cups flour
1 cup salt
4 teaspoons cream of tartar
2 tablespoons vegetable oil
2 cups water
Food coloring

Mix all ingredients together. Place in fry pan and cook until it makes a ball, about 5 minutes. Turn out on plate and cool about 30 minutes. Add desired food coloring to the whole batch or divide it into different colors. Keep in air tight container with lid. DO NOT REFRIGERATE.

Cook over medium heat.

PLAY CLAY

(COOKED)

INGREDIENTS:

1 cup cornstarch
2 cups baking soda
½ cup flour
1-1/3 cups water

Combine dry ingredients in saucepan. Add water and stir constantly over medium heat. When mixture thickens to resemble mashed potatoes, empty onto cool surface and cover with damp cloth until cool (15 minutes).

Knead slightly, mold into desired shapes or objects. Objects air-harden in a few days. Clay remains moist if kept in an airtight container.

NOTES

Devra Berkowitz

Devra Berkowitz is a career physical therapist who has shared her culinary and baking gifts her entire life. Her family, friends, hospital associates, and people in need have all benefited through the years from her cooking and baking skills.

People still ask, "Can I have your recipe?"

Devra is happy to share, as long as the recipe gets passed on and enjoyed.

RECIPE INDEX

5-Minute Chocolate Butter Cream Frosting 103
Angie's Cookies/Biscotti 80
Aunt Ida's Taiglach 108
Baby's Health Crackers 118
Baked Brie 10
Baked Ziti 32
Banana Bread 21
Barbecue Chicken 40
Barbequed Chicken Wings (Hot Wings) 12
Beef Brisket 36
Beef Stew 33
Blackberry Cobbler 99
Blintz Souffle 111
Blueberry Cobbler 98
Blueberry Tea Cake 64
Bread and Butter Pickles 58
Broye du Poitou 97
Buckeyes 94
Carrot Tzimmes 106
Challah 22
Cheese and Apple Spread 11
Cheese Blintzes 112
Chicken Creole 38
Chicken Rice Casserole 44
Chicken Soup 42
Chili Con Carne 34
Chocoholic's Dutch Cocoa Mix 91
Chocolate Cake (Sour Cream) 65
Chocolate Cherry Heart Smart Cookies 96
Chocolate Éclair Cake 68
Cookie Press Cookies 79
Corn Pudding 55

Corned Beef	37
Crab on Toast	11
Cream Cheese Frosting	71
Cream Cheese Frosting	100
Creamed Chicken	60
Dad's Favorite Date Nut Bread	27
Date and Nut Bread	23
Decorator's Frosting	76
Decorator's Fudge Frosting	77
Delicious Coffee Cake	69
Delicious White Cake	72
Dipping Chocolate	93
Eggplant and Ground Meat Parmigiana	47
Fudge Brownies	75
Ginger Snaps	81
Grandma Jane's Taiglach	109
Granny's Biscuits	29
Grape Salad	6
Half Moon Cookies	82
Homemade Play Dough	120
Honey Cake	70
Italian Meatballs	48
Jewish Apple Cake	102
Kentucky Bourbon Balls	92
Knoedle	107
Lemon Flank Steak Skewers	13
Lemon-Blueberry Dutch Baby	95
Luckshion Kugel (Noodles)	110
Marinade for Steak	59
Marinated Mushrooms	53
Matzo Balls	43
Medium White Sauce	45
Molasses Raisin Cookies	83
Mom's Cucumber Salad	57
Mother's Cheese Cake	66

Never Fail Strudel 85
Nut Berry Cheese Ball 17
Passover Sponge Cake 115
Pineapple Cake 71
Plain Crescent Rolls 26
Play Clay 121
Potato Kugel 113
Potato Latkes 114
Pumpkin Pie 89
Red Velvet Layer Cake 100
Refrigerator Cookies 84
Rice Pudding 90
Rich Crescent Rolls 25
Rich Yellow Cake 74
Rugelach (Parve) 86
Rugelach Dough (Dairy) 87
Schnecken 73
Seasoning Mix 52
Shrimp & Grits 62
Soft Buttermilk Dinner Rolls 30
Southern Buttermilk Biscuits 28
Spaghetti Sauce 49
Spanakopita Triangles 14
Strawberry Pie 88
Stuffed Cabbage 54
Swedish Meatballs 16
Sweet Potato Casserole 51
Teething Biscuits 119
Thanksgiving Stuffing 52
Toll House Cookies 78
Tuna Noodle Casserole 50
Vegetable Dip 10
Vegetable Marinade 56
Vienna Christmas Fruit Bread 20
Zucchini Bread 24

NOTES

"A perfect cookbook! A recipe for every occasion from everyday to life's biggest moments. Mom brings her love to our family and to yours."

—Mara, Leah, Lawrence, Seth, Lauren

NOTES